Making and flying kites

If you have already tried to fly a kite, have caught the bug and want to build your own, here are 16 superb flying models to choose from.

This book unlike others shows how to make kites scientifically explaining the aerodynamic principles involved in flying them. It gives detailed yet simple instructions on how to construct the models which range from the simple Malay kite to the Marconi kite and the multicell tetrahedral. The materials needed for making them are easily available and inexpensive.

Kites have fired people's imagination from earliest times to the present day. Fun to build and fly, they have also played an important role in such varied fields as meteorology, air photography and air-sea rescue. Benjamin Franklin used one to prove electricity in the atmosphere, Marconi raised the aerial for his first famous intercontinental radio linkup by kite and the Wright brothers began their experiments into manned flight with box kites.

This book is fully illustrated throughout with drawings and diagrams and will appeal to those of all ages who enjoy making flying models.

Kites: How to Fly Them, How to Build Them

Ambrose Lloyd
Charles Mitchell and
Nicolette Thomas

Holt, Rinehart and Winston
New York

Authors' note

The measurements in inches and feet in this book are not exact conversions of the metric measurements. This has been done on purpose to avoid difficult fractions.

Copyright © 1975 by Ambrose Lloyd, Charles Mitchell, and Nicolette Thomas

Library of Congress Cataloging in Publication Data

Lloyd, Ambrose.
   Kites: How to Fly Them, How to Build Them

   1. Kites. I. Mitchell, Charles, joint author.
II. Thomas, Nicolette, joint author. III. Title.
TL759.L56 1976 796.1'5 75-37220
ISBN 0-03-017476-7
First published in the United States in 1976

Printing set in Great Britain

10 9 8 7 6 5 4 3 2 1

Contents

Section 1

The history of kites   9
How kites fly   24
Flying high – where and how   30
Kite games   39
Kite decoration and attachments   42

Section 2

Materials and structure   51
How to make sixteen different kites   62

Section 1

The history of kites
Fighting kites   11
Ceremonial kites   12
Fishing kites   13
Early European kites   14
Meteorological kites   18
Up to the aeroplane   19
Since the aeroplane   22

How kites fly
At low angle of attack   25
At high angle of attack   27
Stability   28

Flying high – where and how
Where to fly   30
Weather conditions   32
Kite preparation and launching   33
Kite flying   35
Down to earth   37

Kite games

Kite decoration and attachments
Basic rules of decoration   42
Kite attachments   43
Photography from kites   46

The history of kites

Man has only been able to fly powered air-craft since 1903 and lighter-than-air balloons since 1783 so the history of aviation is short. However, aeronautical devices such as the boomerang, the stabilising feathers on arrows and kites have been in use from early times. In fact the kite is such an ancient device that its exact origins are not really known. It seems certain though that it originated in China and the earliest, though ambiguous mention of it appears in a story about Mo Ti, a contemporary of Confucius (c. 500 BC), who built himself a kite shaped like a dove. It took him three years to complete and to his onlookers' scorn crashed on its first trial.

The next, more specific mention of a kite is to be found in the story of Han Hsin about 200 BC. General Han Hsin flew a kite from his own lines over the palace he was besieging. He wanted to calculate the distance between his army and the palace walls so that a tunnel the correct length might be dug to allow his troops to enter. Another story of a later date refers to wind-psalteries – kites equipped with Aeolian harps. Laufer in his *Prehistory of Aviation* tells a story relating to the reign of Emperor Liu Pary: 'A General had resolved to make a last vigorous effort to drive Liu Pary from the throne he had so recently usurped. A battle resulted in the army of the General being hemmed in and threatened with annihilation.

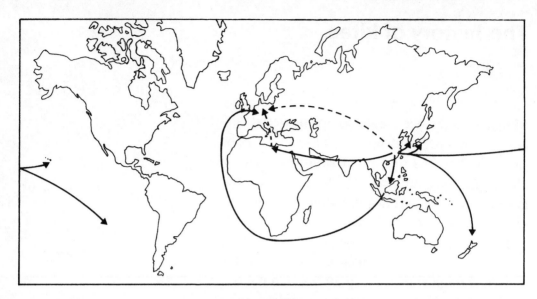

Distribution of the kite before 1600 AD.
(The dotted lines show possible routes by which the kite was introduced to Europe.)

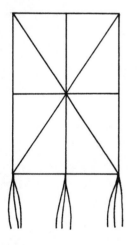

Probable shape of early Chinese kites

At his wits' end to devise a method of escape, he at last conceived the ingenious idea of frightening the enemy by flying kites fitted with Aeolian strings over their camp at the dead of night. The wind was favourable and when all was wrapped in darkness and silence the forces of Liu Pary heard sounds in the air resembling 'FU HAN' Beware of Han! It was their guardian angels, they declared, who were warning them of impending danger, and they fled precipitately, pursued by the General and his army'.

From its source in China the knowledge of kites spread to neighbouring countries – Korea, the Malayan Peninsula, India, Indonesia, Burma, and of course Japan. Kites were flown by the Polynesians even in their remote

Easter Islands settlements. They made their way in stages across Southern Asia and in about the ninth century kites were widespread in Arabia.

The Chinese succeeded in building and flying man-lifting kites, and used them in military lookouts. There is a story of an ingenious thief who managed by means of such a kite to steal gold scales off the dragons adorning the highest pagoda roof of a temple.

As the early Chinese kites were made for practical purposes rather than aesthetic ones they were built on a simple rectangular plan, and it is usually this kite that is depicted in the early paintings of kites. However, as the flying of kites for amusement became more widespread, many intricate and sophisticated, as well as beautiful kites were developed, and the kite became to a degree an end in itself – an art form in which everyone participated. This is why the most beautiful kites come from China.

Fighting kites

The Koreans developed the early rectangular kite into a fast-moving kite made of bamboo and paper. As a tail is a hindrance to mobility it was left off and they rendered the kites partially stable by making a round central hole in the cover, a third of the length of the kite in diameter. During a fight the kite needs to be continually adjusted by the line being released

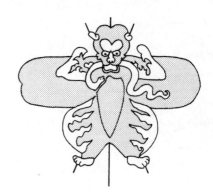

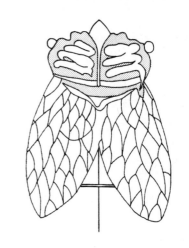

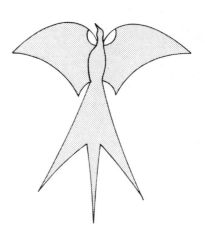

Chinese figure kites

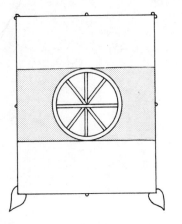

Korean fighting kite

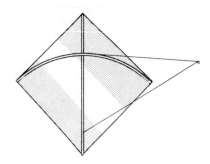

Japanese fighting kite

or tightened, jerked from one side to the other. In this way it can perform remarkable manoeuvres, even flying to windward. In Korea fights are held during the first two weeks of the year. The object is to try to sever your opponent's kite string by crossing it with your own and giving a series of rapid tugs. The line near the kite is armed for this purpose with a coating of glue and powdered glass.

The Japanese fighting kite is probably even faster than the Korean fighter. It, too, flies without a tail and can move rapidly in almost any direction. It is usually very finely made with exact balance and symmetry. Sometimes the bent horizontal spar is tapered at each end to give additional flexibility and the edges of the paper are often reinforced with string. This kite is called by the Japanese 'hata' which means 'flag' and it is commonly coloured red, white and blue – possibly because these are the colours of the Dutch flag and the kite was imported into Japan by the Dutch from the Indies.

Ceremonial kites

On the ninth day of the ninth month of each year, it has become traditional in China to hold a great kite-flying festival called 'kites day'. On this occasion adults and children turn out in great numbers to fly beautiful and varied kites. It is thought that the higher the kite flies, the greater will be the flier's success in life.

The Japanese also hold kite-flying festivals. The best known of these is 'Boys' Day' held on the 5th May. It is an occasion when many kites are flown, principally the paper windsock – in the shape of a carp, which is thought of as a particularly persevering creature, a symbol of the hopes parents have for their sons.

Koreans use ceremonial kites on the fifteenth day of the year when the kite season ends. Tailed kites, with the words 'Bad luck away, Good luck stay' written on them, are flown from hills and when the line is fully out, they are released. Anyone who later finds an abandoned kite will leave it alone for fear of inheriting another man's bad luck. In Southern Polynesia kite flying once formed an essential part of the rituals of sky worship and represented symbolically the souls of gods and heroes. As kite flying was a communication with the heavens, it was essential to build high-flying kites. Considering the materials to hand – leaves, wood bark, rushes, 'tape' (native cloth) and fibre twine – attaining a high performance was no mean feat.

Fishing kites

Leaf kites are used in many of the islands of the Pacific to help catch the long nosed gar-fish. The kites vary greatly, some consisting of leaves with no additional stiffening. Tails were unnecessary with these kites, as the dangling fishing line produced enough drag to stabilise them.

Fishing kite

Early European kites

It has been thought that kites in Europe
originate from trade contact with the East.
First by contact with Arabia in the ninth or
tenth centuries and then in the sixteenth
century through English, Portuguese and
Dutch trading with the Far East. However, it
now seems that there are additional much
older examples of kites in Europe. Clive Hart
in his book *Kites – an historical survey* (Faber
and Faber, 1967) suggests that the dracco – a
windsock shaped like a dragon used as a Roman
military standard after the conquest of Dacia
in AD 105 – was an early forerunner of the
European kite. The windsock acquired a set of
wings by the fourteenth century and so was
able to fly at an angle to the wind like a kite.

Dacian windsock standard or
'dracco'

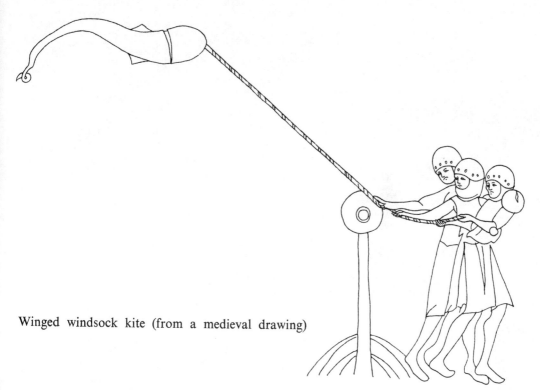

Winged windsock kite (from a medieval drawing)

The next development of the dracco to the Pennon is the leap of invention. The outside shape of a dragon remained but it became a two-dimensional plane supported over two crossed spars.

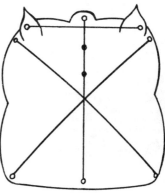

Construction of the Pennon kite

Pennon kite (from a medieval drawing)

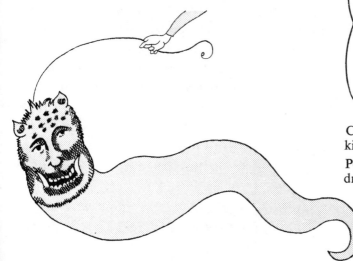

Lozenge-shaped kite

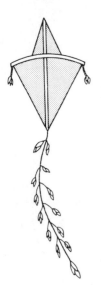

Pear kite

The first kite imported into Europe was the lozenge-shaped kite in the ninth and tenth centuries from Arabia and the pear kite in the sixteenth century from the Far East. The latter became so common and well-known that it is sometimes called the English kite.

As in the East, the plane-surface kite developed many shapes – for example birds, animals and men, as well as hexagonal, octagonal and so-called American 'Barn Door'. As all these kites were inherently unstable without tails, the drive to innovation was towards stability, and it was not until 1890 that the nearly simul-taneous inventions of Eddie and Hargrave re-volutionised kite flying in the West. Eddie invented the dihedral – that is, by bowing the wings back he gave the kite a stabilizing keel. This worked in exactly the same way as the keel on a boat stabilizes the rocking from side

16

to side. It was with ten Eddie kites in train, that is to say from the same line, that the first world height record of 23,385 ft. was set up at Mount Weather, Vermont, U.S.A. in 1910. The present height record was set up by a team of ten boys from Gary, Indiana high school on June 13th 1969. They flew a train of nineteen kites and achieved a height of 35,530 ft using 56,457 ft of line. The flight lasted seven hours and the height was measured by telescopic triangulation.

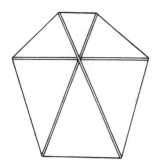

Barn-door kite

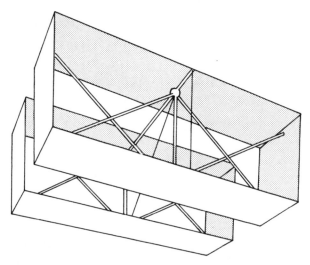

The Hargrave box kite

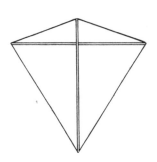

Hargrave's invention, on the other hand, the box kite, was even more stable than Eddie's kite. Hargrave's experiments with kites deserve special mention. He was a thorough and painstaking researcher who first set out to discover and master the aerodynamic principles at work in flight, and he found great interest in successfully developing a soaring kite that would fly past its zenith.

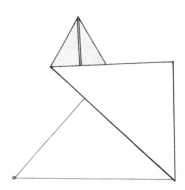

Eddie kites

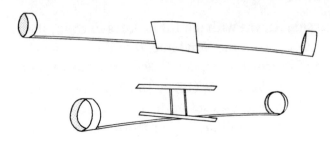

Hargrave's experimental kites

However, in his search for stability he developed a whole series of cellular kite prototypes, which eventually led him to the invention of the box kite. He further extended the box principle by having both the lifting and the stabilizing surfaces rigid cambered aerofoils. This added greatly to the lift, but because of the now critical angle of attack, stability became an even more important factor. Some of the resulting designs still look revolutionary after eighty years.

Meteorological kites

In 1749 Wilson and Melvill made various atmospherical experiments with a train of six pear kites. And Benjamin Franklin by 1752 had made his famous electric kite experiment. He had wished to demonstrate that lightning was an electrical discharge and so flew a kite on a copper line in a thunder-storm. He tied a metal tag – in fact his door key – to the end of the line and a silk ribbon to that, which he held. He then touched the key lightly with his other hand and received an undeniable shock. When he reported his findings to the Royal Society he was laughed at. But subsequent, sometimes painful, experiments by others – even on calm days – proved his theory conclusively.

By 1898 it was practicable to make regular use of kites for meteorological purposes and the U.S. Weather Bureau had seventeen stations taking records in various parts of the country and more stations were opened afterwards. The use of kites was only superseded in the early 1930s by the use of balloons.

Up to the aeroplane

However, by far the most pressing drive to innovation in the West was the idea of flight itself. Whereas the East had explored the spiritual and aesthetic aspects of kite flying, Western man wanted to fly like a bird. Most of the attempts made between 1885 and 1900 at lifting a man off the ground were considered as steps to the development of a flying machine.

Major B.F.S. Baden-Powell – brother of the founder of the Scout movement and later President of the Aeronautical Society – was also deeply interested in man-lifters and he developed the first reliable kite that in a train of four or seven, according to the strength of the wind, could lift a man. Called a 'levitor' it was a simple hexagonal shape which bowed back in the wind producing a dihedral.

Baden-Powell suggested to the British Army that it should adopt his kite for observation purposes, but later, in 1903, when the Army

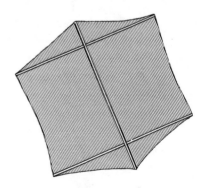

Baden-Powell's 'levitor' kite

Cody's man-lifting kite
A train of Cody man-lifters

took up his suggestion it adopted S.F. Cody's man-lifting kite. This consisted of a twin-celled Hargrave box with added wings for lift. Four kites were flown in train, and then a further kite, from which the observer was suspended seated on a wicker chair, was allowed to travel up the line on a trolley. The observer was able to control the ascent and descent by means of a system of lines and brakes.

Following the publication of the Hargrave's invention many interesting new kites were developed. Perhaps the best known experimenter of this time was Alexander Bell, inventor of the telephone. He modified the Hargrave box to a triangular box kite, which

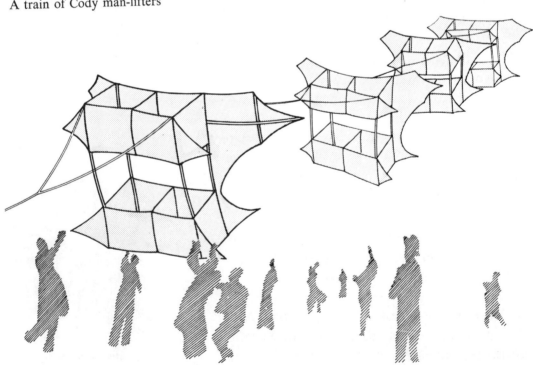

flew with its flat side uppermost. It had more stability – because of the dihedral – and less weight than the original. He then further rationalized the structure to a tetrahedral, that is to say an equal-sided triangular pyramid. This is an inherently strong, stable shape and needs no cross bracing. The structure will fly with any two of its sides covered. However, as far as Bell was concerned its outstanding advantage was the way in which several tetrahedrals could be joined together to form a compound kite. This produced a kite using significantly less material so making the weight to surface ratio even better than in a single-celled version. This is not the case when a Hargrave kite is simply increased in size.

In 1907 Bell made one of the biggest kites ever to fly employing a whole factory to build it. It consisted of 3,393 tetrahedral cells and was equipped with floats. He launched it from a lake with a man aboard towed by a steamer. For several minutes it flew wonderfully, but crashed on landing and it was too expensive to rebuild.

But it was, of course, the Wright brothers who eventually managed to turn a kite into an aeroplane by means of the Hargrave kite and the development of a lightweight motor. They had previously made many carefully controlled experiments with kites and gliders in order to develop ways of controlling the craft and their real break-through came when they consciously chose to develop unstable, high-lift supporting surfaces which were pilot-controlled to keep

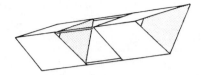

Bell's triangular box kite

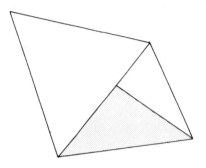

A single cell tetrahedral kite

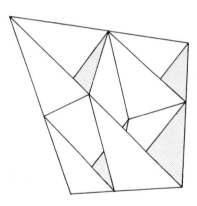

A multicell tetrahedral kite

them flying. An important development was the control obtained by their wing-warping techniques, which adjusted the craft's centre of pressure.

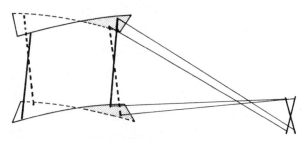

The Wright brothers' wing-warping kite

It was at this point that the story of the aeroplane left the kite world.

Since the aeroplane

Since 1903, in the rush to develop the aeroplane, kites have been all but relegated to their former status. However, some development work has been done since the Second World War. Notably Francis Rogallo of the U.S.A. who invented in 1945 an unstiffened flexible kite called a 'flexi-kite'.

He wished to develop a kite having stability like a parachute with the lift of an aeroplane wing. At first it needed as many as twenty-eight bridle strings, but he was later able to reduce these to four. It is a remarkably good flyer and the curve the wing makes is aerodynamically efficient. Several uses have been made of the

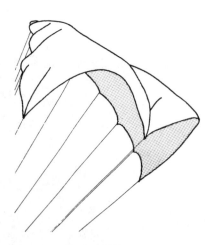

The Rogallo flexi-kite

invention, one of which, the flying jeep, 'the fleep', can operate in rough country carrying loads of up to half a ton.

The flexi-kite used for the 'fleep' was stiffened along its edges and keel. Similarly stiffened examples are used for kite water-skiing and a relatively newly revived, old-fashioned pastime, kite-hanging. This entails using the kite as a hang glider.

Since then various other interesting kites have been developed, such as the 'Sled', a semi-rigid, very simple but effective kite, and the Jalbert 'Para-foil', a frameless, wind-supported aerofoil section. The kite is at present experiencing a revival, and this will undoubtedly give its further development new vigour.

Hang glider

How kites fly

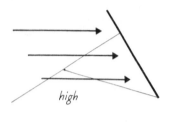

high

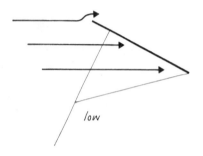

low

Angles of attack

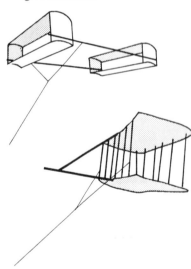

Hargrave's rigid cambered wing kite

The Wright brothers' cambered box kite

We know that kites have been flown since antiquity and that some of their most important design innovations date back over two thousand years. And yet an aerodynamic explanation of how kites fly was not arrived at until this century.

There are two ways in which a kite may be made to fly. At a high angle of attack (i.e. a high angle between the lifting surface and the wind) and at a low angle of attack normal for aerofoils (i.e. between five and fifteen degrees). This latter method has been used by only a few people such as Hargrave and the Wright brothers in their cambered surface box kites.

A kite depends not only on the wind to give it lift, but also on the kite line to keep it under pressure in the wind. The line keeps the kite relatively still while the air rushes past, in contrast to an aeroplane which moves forward through the air itself. In both cases the relative wind speed is the same.

To obtain lift from the wind, the kite cover must have a degree of wind resistance or 'wind proofing'. The wind must be forced to pass around the cover, not allowed to blow through it. On occasions, though, in a high wind, it often helps a kite's stability to reduce its wind resistance by using a permeable cover material such as cotton, rather than say P.V.C. sheet.

At low angle of attack

Those special kites that fly at a low angle of attack obtain their lift like aeroplanes by changing the pressure of the air as it passes over the lifting surfaces. This happens following Bernouilli's principle, which states that the pressure of a fluid (liquids or gases) decreases as its speed increases and vice versa. By angling the kite cover into the wind, the air passing over its top surface, is induced to go faster than the air passing around the bottom surface. Thus there is greater pressure on the lower surface than the upper one and the kite moves upwards to equalize the discrepancy.

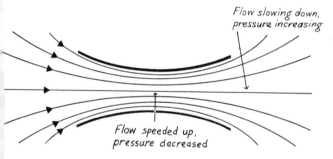

Flow slowing down, pressure increasing

Flow speeded up, pressure decreased

Bernouilli's principle

However, there are complicating factors. A flat plane has the disadvantage of tending to break-up the wind into swirls and backwashes, i.e. turbulence. This turbulence slows the air passing over the top surface and so considerably reduces the lift and greatly increases its drag. If the air is eased over the top surface by means of streamlining, it will flow smoothly and so produce its lift with little drag.

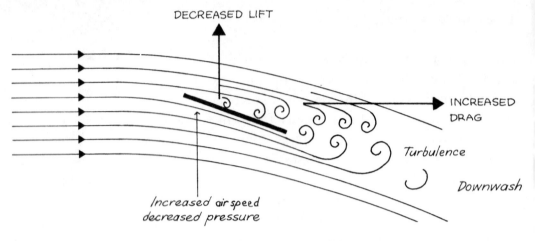

Air flow over a flat plane

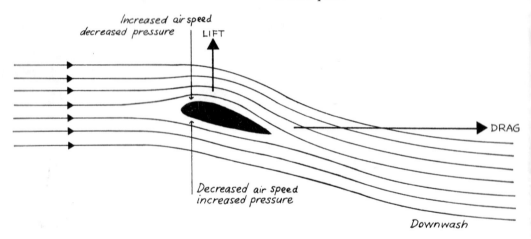

Air flow over an aerofoil inclined at a low angle

The angle of attack a kite assumes is also connected to both lift and turbulence. Starting from an angle of about five degrees to the horizontal, every increase towards the vertical will make the air move faster over the top surface and so increase its lift but only to a certain point. At about fifteen degrees, the air refuses to be bent around any further and it starts breaking-up into turbulence; the lift falls off rapidly and produces stall.

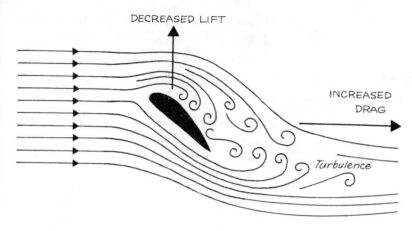

Turbulent air flow over aerofoil inclined
at a high angle

At high angle of attack

A normal kite flies in a somewhat different
manner to that described above. It is flown at a
high angle of attack which an aeroplane would
find almost impossible to maintain. However,
the kite line prevents the kite from being
pushed backwards by the increased wind resistance and consequent drag. The air passing
over the top surface of the kite is turbulent and
so not able to contribute much to the kite's
lift. The air on the lower surface, though, is
being deflected downwards and pressed against
the kite. This will give it an increased pressure
and so cause it to lift.

The bridle can be adjusted to so distribute the
pressure of the wind on the kite cover that it
will maintain an efficient angle of attack. The
nearer to the horizontal this is, the greater the
lift. The buffetting of the turbulence behind it is
what makes a flat kite unstable.

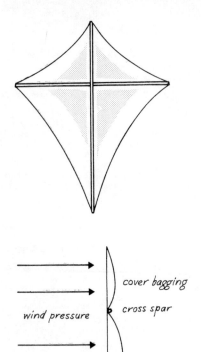

In actual fact the surfaces of a normal kite are not quite flat; if they were, the kite would be very unstable. The kite cover is pressed by the wind into curved depressions between the spars, and the surfaces become somewhat cambered as in an aerofoil. This helps to ease the air over the top surface with the resulting reduction of turbulence and increase of lift. Also the spars, which will project a little, act as stabilizing keels.

wind pressure

cover bagging

cross spar

Wind bagging on a flat surface

Stability

A kite may be given an extra stability in the following ways:

Tails – tails do not, as one would expect, stabilize a kite by adding weight. They add drag. The tail should weigh very little, but when it streams out behind the kite, by dragging in the wind it gives an additional pull backwards that helps keep the kite face on to the wind. Additional weight would only 'dampen' the kite's movement and hinder its lift. Long tails also help to stabilize the kite's movement from side to side by taking up the snaking motion a little while after the kite and so counteracting this movement.

Dihedrals – a kite is said to have a dihedral when it is bowed back from the wind making a central keel. As one side of the kite tips backwards, it receives less wind pressure, while the other side will take up a position of increased wind pressure, and according to the natural law of equalization the two pressures will force the kite to move back into equilibrium.

Side surfaces – box kites have side surfaces to give them stability, like rudders. This device is so successful that a box kite in a heavy puff of wind will not be pushed backwards under strain to a position of greater wind resistance and less lift, but will move towards the horizontal assuming a steady angle of least resistance to the wind and still retain some of its lift. It is said then to 'lie on the wind'. When a box kite is flown flat side on to the wind, it will have two lifting surfaces and two stabilizing surfaces. If it is flown edge on to the wind, all the surfaces assume the dual function of lifting and stabilizing.

And in a triangular box kite, which is flown edge on to the wind, the front two surfaces provide stability (with the added stability of presenting a dihedral to the wind), and the back surface provides lift.

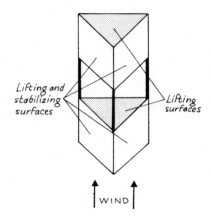

Purpose of surfaces of triangular box kite

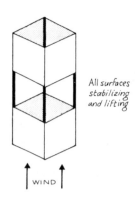

Purpose of surfaces of square box kite

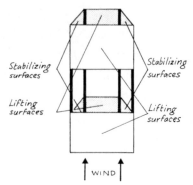

Purpose of surfaces of oblong box kite

Flying high Where and how

Where to fly

Flying kites in heavily built-up areas is hazard-ous. Apart from the obvious limitations of lack of open space, air disturbance caused by buildings and traffic makes launching a kite difficult. For the same reasons it is not easy to launch a kite in a heavily forested area. But whereas it is possible to climb a tree, rescuing a kite from a stranger's roof-top requires the kite flyer to brave the house-holder's dis-belief, ridicule, suspicion and sometimes even scorn.

The best places for launching a kite:

A flat field

The windward side of a hill

Near the sea or a lake

If you wish to fly a kite from the top of a hill you should launch it on the windward side, a few feet below the lip of the hill rather than from the top itself. There will be a stronger upward draught there than on the crest. The best winds

Where and when not to fly a kite:

Near a road or railway

Near overhead power cables

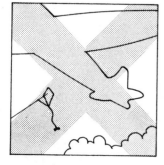

Within five miles of an airport

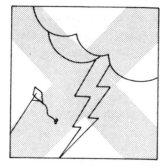

In a thunderstorm

for flying kites are those with speeds of 5 to 25 knots. It is a good idea to have a selection of kites, built to fly in different weathers, just as sailors have suits of sail for various weathers. A box or multiple-plane kite will fly well in wild, blustery weather. The surfaces angled to the wind act like rudders, giving it stability. On the other hand, a flat bird-like kite has maximum lift and so will rise in the slightest of winds – in fact, the concessions to lift in its design often make it necessary to attach a tail to give it stability.

Weather conditions

In the interests of deciding when to fly, and choosing a suitable kite, it is useful to know a little about weather forecasting. Attention to weather is as much a part of the preparation and build-up to successful kite flying, as is the attention the kite should receive.

Beaufort Scale

Beaufort force	Description	Effects on land	Wind speed/knots	Type of kite suitable
0	Calm	Smoke rises vertically.	Less than 1	
1	Light breeze	Wind direction shown by smoke drift, but not strong enough to turn wind vanes.	1–3	Only the lightest small kites with maximum lift.
2	Light wind	Wind felt on face. Leaves rustle. Wind vanes respond to wind.	4–6	Lightweight small and medium sized kites.
3	Gentle wind	Leaves and small twigs in constant motion. Wind extends light flags.	7–10	Perfect for most kites except very heavy.
4	Moderate wind	Raises dust and paper. Moves small branches.	11–15	Medium and large kites. Best for Box kites.
5	Fresh wind	Small trees begin to sway.	16–21	Strong, sturdy kites with good stability.
6	Strong wind	Large branches in motion. Telegraph wires hum. Umbrellas difficult.	22–27	Very strong kites only.

Kite preparation and launching

Checking the balance, making adjustments to tensions, mending worn pockets, and generally making sure that the kite is airworthy is important and a kind of insurance against the moment when you're unfolding your kite surrounded by an audience curious to see what's happening. It's your judgement at stake after all!

When you arrive at your chosen launching site, resist the temptation to run frantically off across the field, hoping that the kite will rise up gloriously behind you. This won't happen. The kite is more likely to bump along the ground behind you, causing itself damage. If you find that you have to run to launch a kite, you're flying the wrong kite for the weather, so choose a different model.

Before launching a kite, let out a little line and throw the kite lightly up into the air to check its balance. This is the time to make adjustments to the bridle's angle of incline and to the length of the tail before finally offering the kite to the wind. Correct adjustments to the bridle are essential to successful and enjoyable kite flying.

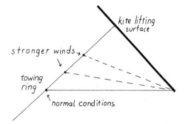

Bridle adjustment for stronger winds

If the wind is light and you are using a kite reel it is possible to loft the kite by means of 'winching'. After launching the kite let the line run slack until the kite flutters almost to the ground. Then reel in quickly so that the kite soars up into the air. When it reaches the apex of its curve allow the line to run slack again until the kite drops near the ground. Then once again reel in quickly. Do this repeatedly until the kite has reached the height at which you wish it to fly. This 'winching' will allow the kite to achieve good height and distance and may carry it to a height where there is more wind.

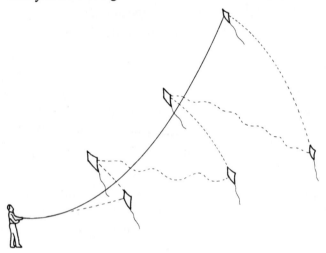

Lofting a kite by 'winching'

If you have a helper, another way of launching a kite in light winds is to unroll about 25m (80 ft). of line and have your helper hold the kite as high above his head as he can. If the kite has a tail it should stretch out behind him. In this position it will help balance the kite as it rises into the air. As your helper releases the kite, move backwards until the kite begins to rise, then slowly let out more line.

There is a rule that applies to all helpers, whether they be friends, wives, fathers, children, or strangers. That is: they can't help it. So keep your instructions to them clear, and your recriminations to yourself.

It is important not to let the line out too quickly when launching or the kite will fall. The stronger the breeze, the faster the line may be released. If the wind is strong enough and you still have difficulty in getting the kite to rise, or find that it dances from side to side, try re-adjusting the bridle or changing the length of the tail.

Limits to which you can reel out line depend on the size of the kite, the force of the wind, and the strength of the line. As you can buy nylon line in various weights, a kite should be considered in the condition of maximum wind resistance, and the line chosen accordingly. The criterion, though, in your choice should be that the less weight the kite is carrying the better. It is wise to realise how quickly weather, and therefore flying conditions, can change, and so be prepared to bring down the kite and change not only the thickness of the line but also the type of kite.

Kite flying

When the kite has been launched and lofted to a reasonable height you have a chance to show your skill. It's not just a question of standing still with a line in your hand, there's more to it than that. The kite will need your attention still. Remember that the wind is never constant and can increase, drop, or change its direction very quickly, affecting the way the kite flies. You will need to make small corrective pulls on the line to keep the kite flying well.

Flying high
Suggested types of kite and line for different winds

Weather	Breaking strain of line	Type of kite
Calm	20 lb	Hexagonal kite Figure kites (paper)
Gentle wind	30 lb	8-pt Star kite Marconi kite Hexagonal kite Nagasaki kite Sled kite Korean fighter Figure kites
Moderate wind	50 lb	Triangular box 8-pt Star kite Marconi kite Aeroplane kite Nagasaki kite Sled kite Korean fighter
Strong wind	100 lb	Aeroplane kite Triangular box Sled kite Box kite

But so long as you keep constant vigilance this is the best part of kite flying. This is the culmination of all the measuring, cutting and joining, the end of the worrying about whether it will fly or not. This moment, when your kite is up there, is what it was all for. Just to sit and watch your kite floating, seemingly without effort, on an ocean of air, is a wonderful experience.

If there are other people flying kites nearby, be careful not to interfere with them. Carelessly flown kites cause damage and frayed tempers. If they are willing, you could join other flyers in a competition to see whose kite flies highest or is the most manoeuvrable. There are a few suggested games to play with kites on page 39.

Down to earth

Landing a kite can be one of the most difficult parts of kite flying. In a strong steady breeze, a skilful kite flyer can bring the kite in to his hand like an obedient falcon, without letting it touch the ground. In a high wind, even a kite brought in slowly and carefully can crash at the last moment, so special attention must be paid. If you have a helper, ask him to walk out along the line towards the kite, pulling the line down as he goes. When he reaches a distance from you of about 35m (100 ft), he should stop and hold the line, taking the tension off it while you walk towards him reeling in. Do this repeatedly until the kite is down. If no-one is available or willing to help, you can do much to relieve the tension on the line by walking towards the kite and reeling in at the same time. The kite will be easier to bring down in a light wind. The safest way of landing it will be to reel in slowly and steadily until the kite is within a few yards of you and then let the line go entirely slack so that the kite drops lightly to the ground.

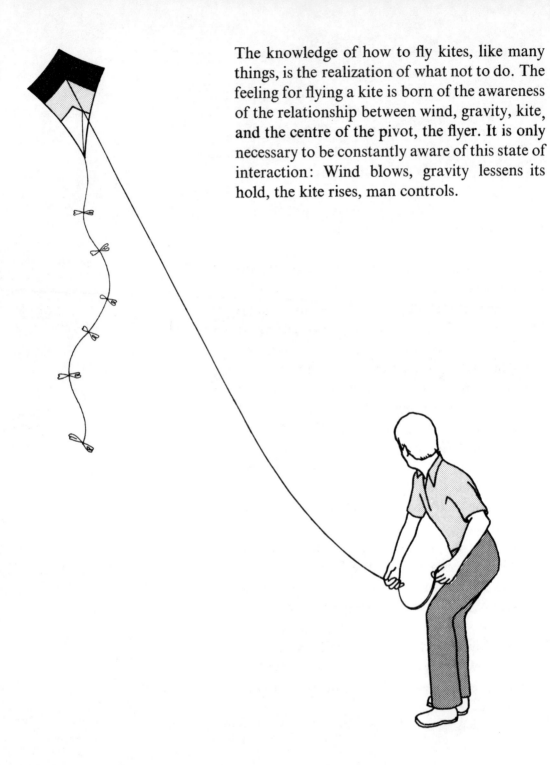

The knowledge of how to fly kites, like many things, is the realization of what not to do. The feeling for flying a kite is born of the awareness of the relationship between wind, gravity, kite, and the centre of the pivot, the flyer. It is only necessary to be constantly aware of this state of interaction: Wind blows, gravity lessens its hold, the kite rises, man controls.

Kite games

Kite flying, essentially a solitary activity, takes on a new dimension when two or more people fly. Contests, far more common in the East, may be held on special kite flying days, such as Boy's Day in Japan. Kites are usually divided into classes for this purpose to match flying abilities, thus

Flat kites with tails.
Bow kites without tails.
Multiplane kites.

Then various performance contests may be held, such as

Best height on given length of line.
Most stable kite.
Quickest riser in set time.

Kite fighting, the most ancient of all kite games, is still an exhilarating sport, requiring great skill. Fighting has been central to most kite-flying contests in the East, and in the past commanded widespread participation and a large following. This was so great in Malaya, that the government there banned all kite fights for fear of violence.

Although Eastern kite fighting entailed the use of knives and glass coated lines, it is possible to have just as skilful and exciting fights with unarmed manoeuvres – which saves on kites. Two contestants raise kites of the same class, size and weight to an agreed height and

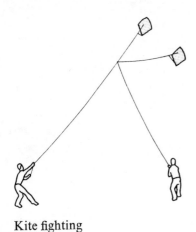

Kite fighting

the battle commences. The manoeuvre that hooks the opponent's kite out of the sky may go like this: 'A' manoeuvres his kite until it lies slightly below his opponent's, then rapidly hauls in causing his kite to rise up under his opponent's line. He continues to make his kite rise until he has carried his opponent's line high enough to interfere with the tension on his kite. A kite with no tension on its line will lose its lift and fall. So his opponent is forced to haul in line frantically. Every time a kite loses purchase on the air like this, the contestant loses one of five lives.

Here are two other games:

Riddle game

Riddle game

1. Each team consists of two people.
2. Any number of teams can play.
3. Each team has one kite with say 65m (200ft) of line and a pencil.
4. The person with the kite stands 65m (200ft) upwind from his partner who is equipped with the pencil.
5. A written riddle is given to the kite flyer.
6. He attaches the riddle to his kite and launches it to his partner.
7. His partner catches the kite and writes his answer to the riddle on the paper.
8. With his partner's help, the flyer again launches the kite and tows it back towards himself.
9. If the answer is not correct, the procedure is repeated, with the kite being flown back and

forth between the two partners until they get
the answer correct.
10. The first team to produce the right answer
wins.

Bulldog Drummond

This is a group game derived from the ancient
game IT.
1. Any number of kite flyers stand in a group
and launch their kites.
2. The last person to loft his kite satisfactorily
is IT.
3. IT then attempts to touch other kites with
his own.
4. Those whose kites are touched, join IT in
pursuing the rest.
5. The last person whose kite is touched is the
winner.

Kite decoration and attachments

Designing and decorating kites is both fun and creative. It offers infinite scope for individual expression and originality. Within the basic range of the sixteen different principles of kite design illustrated in section two, there are any number of variations possible. In fact, most kite designs derive from one of these basic principles. It is therefore possible to develop original kites, designing your own structural system by using an appropriate basic form and applying the rules of symmetry and balance. And there are as many ways of decorating them as there are few limiting rules.

Basic rules of decoration

1. Structure

An important design consideration is the relationship between the structural pattern and the decoration of the kite. The decoration, figurative or abstract, should always relate strongly to the kite's basic form. Some Japanese kites take this ideal to superb extremes with the decoration dictating the form.

2. Design

There is one particular graphic consideration to keep in mind. You should remember that the design on the kite will be seen at a distance

Japanese kite

and so should be simple and bold in general layout, but could have delicate detailing within the bold outlines.

3. Colour

The distance also affects the way in which colours are perceived – they tend to lose their strength, and this together with the silhouetting effect of the kite against the light sky makes the colours seem darker and weaker. To compensate you should use strong, clear colours, containing as little grey as possible. Movement can be employed as a strong visual element – fluttering edges, waving fronds, revolving discs, and even more simply, on a 3-dimensional kite like a box, the movement of one plane in front of another. This effect may be heightened by the use of vivid complementary colours against each other, (blue and orange; red and green; etc.), or even using a simplified moiré pattern on transparent P.V.C.

Japanese kite

Malaysian figure kite

Kite attachments

Here is a list of kite attachments which can be fun but must also obey the rules of symmetry and balance – for example you must attach an equal number of tassels to each side of the kite otherwise it will fly lopsidedly.

Tails
bunched
folded
tasselated

43

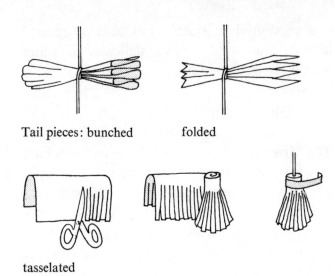

Tail pieces: bunched   folded

tasselated

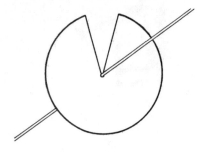

Paper messenger

Festoonings – almost anything that is light and decorative:
paper streamers
tinsel
feathers
dried grasses/leaves

Lights – weight is the problem here – don't overload the kite with battery and bulb circuits, and remember balance. But lights can produce an exciting effect at night.

Fireworks – sparklers are best, with a fuse to enable the kite to rise high before they ignite, but consider well the fire-risk both to your kite and other's property.

Parachute – this is blown up the kite line and when the line is jerked the messenger releases the parachute and it floats gently down.

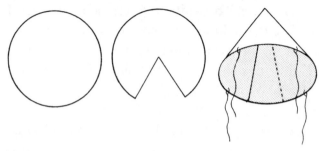

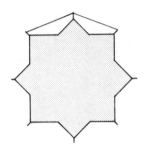

Parachute
(a) Cut circle of soft tissue paper
(b) Cut out small wedge shaped piece
(c) Lightly paste the two edges together to make cone shape. Attach four 60 cm (2 ft) long threads at equal intervals round the rim

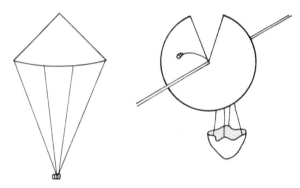

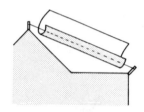

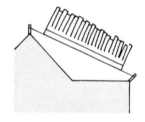

(d) Hold parachute tip and knot threads together at bottom. Attach small weight
(e) Fix parachute and messenger to kite line as shown.

Buzzer

Music attachments

Buzzers – take a strip of paper and glue one edge round a string or spar. Cut a fringe in the strip so that it will vibrate in the wind, creating a buzzing noise.

Hummers – add a bowed spar to the back of the kite. The bow should be tied with piano-wire or a guitar string. It is possible to fit several hummers to one kite so that a harmony is produced.

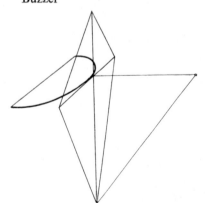

Hummer

45

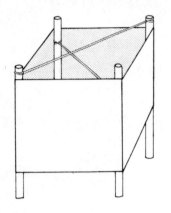

Harp

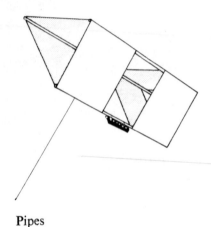

Pipes

Harps – on a box-kite, stretch metal strings of different thicknesses across one or both ends without allowing them to touch each other. The strings will vibrate in the wind producing a pleasant sound.

Pipes – tie 'penny-whistles' or pan-pipes to one of the spars, making sure that the mouth-pieces are facing into the wind.

Photography from kites

It is possible, by means of a camera suspended from the frame, to use a kite for the purpose of aerial photography. This was successfully done at the turn of the century by meteorologists and army technicians wishing to observe the enemy without endangering lives. Photography from aeroplanes has largely made the technique outmoded, but there are still instances where a photograph taken from a kite can be a better (and less expensive) method than photographs taken from an aeroplane – photographing a house in a built-up area for instance. For the keen photographer it can be an interesting, and sometimes surprising experience.

When first experimenting with kite photography, it would be wise to use a cheap camera until you have mastered the skills involved. Make sure that the camera is securely attached to the frame and is pointing in the right direction for the photographs you wish to take. When positioning the camera on the frame remember that the kite dips forward in flight. Early experimenters used various ingenious devices for releasing the shutters of their cameras, including slow-burning fuses and explosions. You might like to experiment with some of these methods, or even devise your own. A simple device is to arrange a rubber-band so that it will jerk the shutter across or release it, depending on the type of camera you are using. Then relieve the shutter from the pull of the rubber-band by a string to which a fuse is attached. Alternatively, attach a time-release mechanism to the camera, or, if you are lucky enough to have one, use a motor-driven camera that will automatically take photographs at pre-set time intervals.

Glossary diagrams

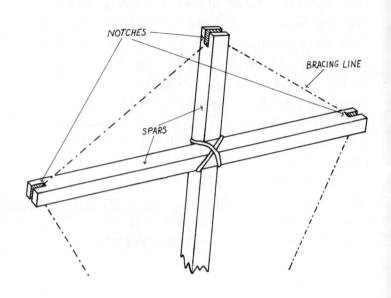

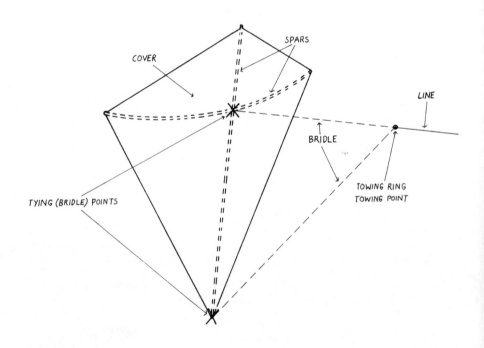

Section 2

Materials and structure

Materials   51
Kite construction   56

Sixteen kites to make

Malay kite   62
Sled kite   64
Hexagonal kite   66
Umbrella kite   68
Eight-pointed star   70
Korean kite   72
Japanese kite   74
Nagasaki fighting kite   76
Aeroplane kite   78
Pyramid kite   80
Box kite   82
Bird kite   84
Marconi kite   86
Triangulated box kite   88
Conyne kite   90
Multicell tetrahedral kite   93

Material	Lightness	Wind resistance	Ease of use	Hardwearing
Silk	+	√	×	√
Silk substitute	√	○	×	√
Lightweight nylon	√	○	×	√
Closely woven cotton	○	○	○	√
P.V.C. sheet	√	+	+	√
Spinnaker sail	+	√	○	+
Fibrous tissue	√	○	√	○
Tissue paper	√	○	√	×
Rice paper	√	○	√	×
Brown wrapping paper	○	○	√	○
Polystyrene tiles	+	+	√	×
Crepe paper	○	○	√	○

Key
Very good   +
Good   √
Moderate   ○
Poor   ×

Materials

Cover materials

The selection of materials for making a kite will depend not only on their suitability but also on availability and cost. Silk, for instance, is a practical material to use for covers being light and strong, but is expensive. Whereas brown wrapping paper, not only a cheap and a commonly available material, is also strong and light enough to make a good cover.

Covers can, and have been made of such widely differing materials as polystyrene, spinnaker sail, old newspaper, leaves and even old umbrella covers. It might be helpful to list some of the more readily available and suitable materials under the criteria they should fulfil: see table opposite.

Spars

Light square-section hardwood, or softwood, is a particularly good material for kite spars provided it is free from knots and defects. It has the advantage of being easily obtainable – both from model shops and timber merchants.

Most kites in this book use square-section spars but bamboo can easily be substituted if more easily obtained. If bamboo is used it is important that corresponding struts on the kite are of exactly the same thickness and strength so that the kite is balanced. The pieces may need some work on them shaving off irregularities with a sharp knife before they are ready to use. Not only is bamboo a strong, flexible wood, but the fact that it is hollow makes it lighter than solid timber. Another useful quality of bamboo is that it can be bent without breaking, and the bend may be fixed without tying by waving the bent bamboo strip over a small flame and then allowing it to cool.

Most Chinese and Japanese kites use bent bamboo strips and certainly this is the material you should use for making complicated small kites such as insect kites. In the West the best way of obtaining this form of bamboo is to buy a bamboo slatted dinner mat or window blind as this saves all the hard work needed to prepare the material.

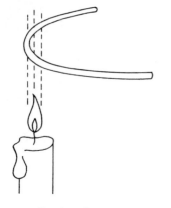

Bending bamboo

Thin-walled aluminium and duranium alloy tubes have a particularly good strength/weight ratio. They do, however, have their drawbacks, their relatively high cost not least among them. They also need some ingenuity to join together. Welding, for instance, is an obvious choice; but not many people have access to the equipment needed. A screw-fix is probably one of the most effective ways of joining, and this has the added advantage of being demountable. It should be said that a kite made with this kind of care and with such high performance materials as alloy tube and spinnaker sail will result in a superb soaring machine.

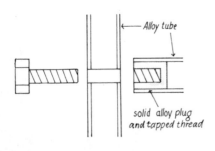

Alloy tube

solid alloy plug and tapped thread

Cross-section of screw-fix method of joining alloy tubes

Adhesives

Paper and Tissue:
Tissue paste
Home-made flour paste
Petroleum based glue
Double-sided adhesive tape.

Cloth (if not sewn):
Light rubber based glues
Vinyl-based glues

P.V.C. Sheet:
Adhesive tape
Welder. Where many P.V.C. kites are to be made, at a school for example, it might be economical to buy a small welding machine.

Line

Lightweight nylon line is the cheapest and most practical type of line available and can be used for all purposes. It can be obtained in many weights and thicknesses. For small kites choose a line with a breaking strain of 25 or 50 lbs. For large kites a line with a breaking strain of 95 to 200 lbs. is best. Alternatively fishing line is a good material to use and has the advantage of being readily available. Ordinary household string can be used but it is sometimes rather heavy for a small kite. Never use a wire because this can conduct electricity from the atmosphere.

Tools

Very few tools are required for successful kite making. The following list contains all that is needed for making the kites illustrated in this book:

Fine saw – dovetail or hacksaw
Scissors
Long ruler
Large-eyed needle
Craft knife
Dress-making pins

Flying accessories

It is useful to have the following items with you when flying your kite, either to aid your flying or to make small repairs.
– Reel or winding bobbin.
– Gloves. In strong winds the line can become very difficult to hold, and can give severe and painful hand burns. So wear strong gloves. It is possible to buy gardening gloves quite cheaply and these are good for kite flying.
– Scissors or a knife.
– Needle and cotton (for repairing pockets).
– Adhesive tape.

Reels

It is possible to make a kite fly to moderate heights with no other equipment than a stick on which to wind the string or line. However, to fly a kite to a great height and to bring it successfully back to earth is much easier if you have a reel. Winding in without a reel becomes a chore, taking a long time, and is not much fun. A reel overcomes this difficulty and is so easy to make that any keen kite-flier should make one. The only tool you'll need apart from those already mentioned is a drill.

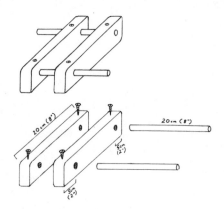

Winding bobbin

A winding bobbin is easier to make than a reel and while not being so good for a long line is considerably better than a stick.

Winding bobbin.
(The handles are secured by screws)

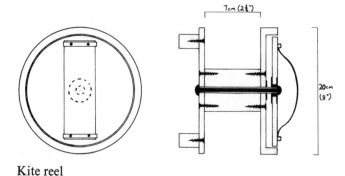

Kite reel

Kite construction

The instructions on how to make the kites in this section follow a step by step sequence. First we show a drawing of the finished kite to show you how it should look, with dimensions in centimetres and inches. We also give a cutting list of the materials to be used, like the list of ingredients in a recipe for a cake.

In the set of diagrams, the kite skeleton or structure is shown first; then the lengths of spars required; this is followed by the joints or tying of the spars. The flat shape of the cover with dimensions is shown next; then how to seam or edge it; then its construction and pockets etc. We then show how the frame and the cover fit together and are secured. And finally the way in which the bridle is tied.

The sixteen kites we have chosen represent a cross-section of all the basically different types of kite available and they are arranged in order of complexity of construction. The simple 'Malay' is therefore first and the complex Multicell Tetrahedral kite last.

Some of the main elements of construction common to all models are listed below. These should be studied carefully before you attempt to make any of the kites.

Notches

If a kite frame requires a bracing line, the ends of the spars will need to be notched. To make a notch saw a narrow slot $\frac{1}{2}$cm ($\frac{1}{4}''$) deep at the end of the spar. Alternatively for bamboo cut a V-shaped notch also $\frac{1}{2}$cm ($\frac{1}{4}''$) deep.

Cross-bracing

To join two cross-spars, place the spars together to the angle required and hold them in place. Wind string tightly round the crossing point and hold it, there is no need to tie a knot. When enough string to hold the spars securely has been used (10 or 12 turns should be enough) cover the joint with quick-drying glue for a really secure joint.

If there are three spars crossing over at one point, join two as above and then add the third. Where four spars cross, make two sets of two and then join these together in the same way.

Knots

The following knots and tying methods are used:

(a) V-shaped notch for bamboo
(b) Slot notch for square-section hardwood/softwood
(c) Other types of notches required for some kites

Cross bracing

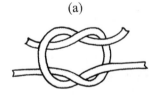

(a)

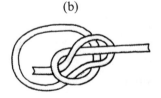

(b)

(a) *Reef knot*: a general purpose knot
(b) *Bowline*: useful and reliable for tying kite lines to bridle

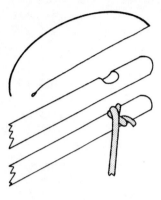

Bowing

Bowing

Some kites require a bowed surface to give them stability. To bow a spar cut a notch 1cm ($\frac{1}{2}''$) from each end of the spar before attaching the cover. After the cover has been attached to the frame cut a piece of string a little longer than the spar that is to be bowed. Lie the kite face down and tie the string to one end using the notch to stop the string slipping along the spar. Bend the spar gently to the required curve and tie the string to the notch at the other end of the spar.

Covers

The best and simplest method of cutting out a kite's cover is to place the finished kite frame on to the cover material (making sure that the material is laid flat, without folds or creases). Then, using the frame as a template, mark round its edge with chalk or a felt pen. It is important to leave an extra 2cm ($\frac{3}{4}''$) hem all round for fixing the cover to the frame. If a cloth cover is being used make sure that the direction of the weave is from top to bottom and side to side, and in no other direction.

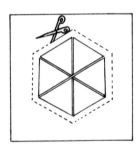
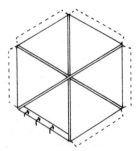

Cutting and attaching cover

When using glue, read the instructions on the container to find out the approximate drying time. Don't use too much glue, it doesn't make the kite any more efficient. The best glues for attaching a cover to the frame are 'impact' adhesives, where after the glue has been spread on the surfaces, the two parts are set aside to dry slightly, and are then pressed firmly to-gether, binding immediately.

If the cover is to be sewn, it is best to use a sewing machine for a neater and stronger join.

In some cases, particularly large kites designed to fly in heavy winds, it is better to nail the cloth cover to the frame with small tacks. Do this by turning the hem once round a spar and then place tacks at regular intervals down the whole length of the spar.

Bridles

The short strings from the kite to the main flying line are called the bridle. The function of the bridle is to hold the kite at the correct angle to the wind while it is flying.

Some kites, a box kite for example, will fly quite well without a bridle, the tying point being carefully chosen so that the wind and gravitational forces maintain a satisfactory flying angle. Most kites, however, require a 2-, 3- or 4-leg bridle.

To make the bridle, strengthen the cover at the points shown on the individual kite instruc-tions. This may be done with paper re-inforcing circles on paper kites, adhesive tape on P.V.C. covers, and extra squares of material on cloth covers. Pierce the strengthened cover and tie the bridle string round the spar behind. The instructions for each individual kite will tell

Looping the string through the towing ring

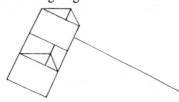

No bridle

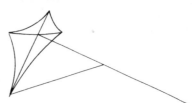

2-leg bridle

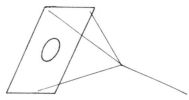

3-leg bridle

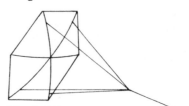

4-leg bridle

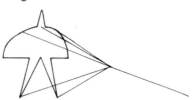

5-leg bridle

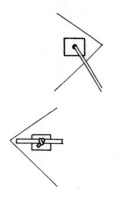

Attaching bridle to tying point

you how long that string should be.

For a two-leg bridle, attach one end of the string to one of the tying points and loop (see diagram) the string through a small metal towing ring (a curtain ring or small washer is ideal) before tying the other end down. For a three-leg bridle, use two lengths of string, one of which is tied to the ring itself. If a four-leg bridle is required, use two crossing strings, looping them both through the towing ring.

The position of the towing ring can be adjusted by sliding it along the strings. The ring will remain in position when the line and bridle are made taut.

The kite should lean forward into the wind. If the towing point is too low, the kite will fly vertically and will not rise; if it is too high, the kite will fly at too low an angle and will flutter and behave in a generally erratic manner. In strong winds the kite generally needs to fly at a lower angle of attack, 'flatter' to the ground. So the towing-ring should be adjusted for weather conditions before each flight. The position of towing-rings in all the construction diagrams is set for moderate wind conditions.

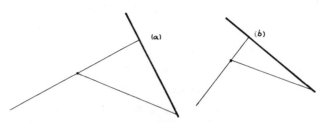

Bridle for normal wind conditions
The bridle is tied higher for strong winds

Tails

When making tails, it is important to remember that it is length and not weight that helps balance a kite. Generally a tail should be five times the height of the kite frame to give it proper stability, although this length may need varying a little for different conditions.

MALAY KITE

Although a traditional Eastern kite, it was developed in the West by Eddie in the late nineteenth century and was used extensively in meteorological research of the upper atmosphere, determining temperatures and pressure. It flies very well in moderate and high winds.

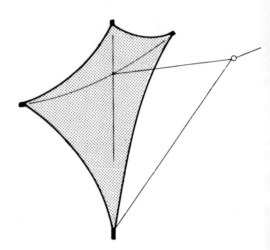

Materials required

Spars—square section hardwood or softwood
One spar 90cm (36 in) × 0·6cm (¼ in)
One spar 84cm (33 in) × 0·6cm (¼ in)

Cover 90cm (36 in) × 90cm (36 in)
Lightweight cloth or tissue paper or crepe paper

Line
Glue
Towing ring

Conversions
120cm = 48 in
90cm = 36 in
84cm = 33 in
75cm = 30 in
15cm = 6 in
7·5cm = 3 in
5cm   = 2 in

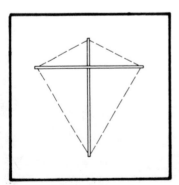

Structural form

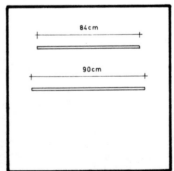

Measure spars carefully

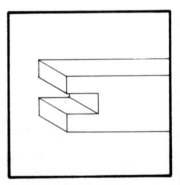

Notch ends of both spars

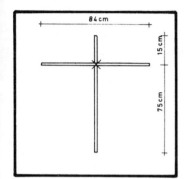

Tie short spar to spine

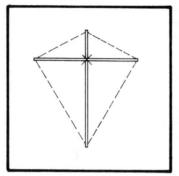

Tie line round frame

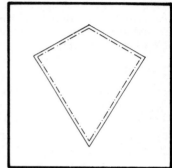

Cut out cover allowing hem all round

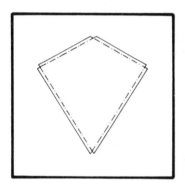

Nick corners of hem to allow turning

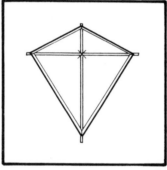

Attach cover to frame by turning and glueing down hem

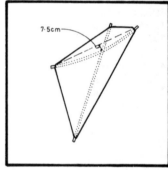

Tie line along back of cross-spar and tighten to bow

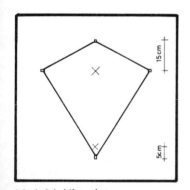

Mark 2 bridle points

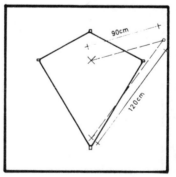

Fix 2-leg bridle

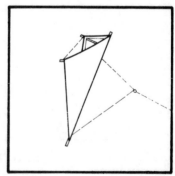

Position for launching

SLED KITE

This most recently designed kite was
first developed in America. It came
from experiments for improving parachutes.
Flies well in all winds.

Materials required

Spars—square section hardwood
or softwood or bamboo
Two spars 90cm (36 in) × 0·6cm ($\frac{1}{4}$ in)

Cover 100cm (40 in) × 100cm (40 in)
200 Gauge Polythene or PVC

Adhesive tape
Metal eyelets
Line

Conversions

360cm = 12 ft
180cm = 6 ft
90cm = 36 in
50cm = 20 in
45cm = 18 in
40cm = 16 in
25cm = 10 in
7·5cm = 3 in

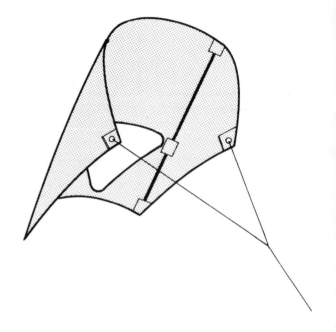

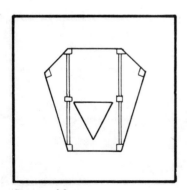

Structural form

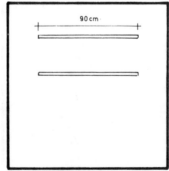

Measure spars carefully

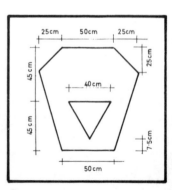

Cut out cover

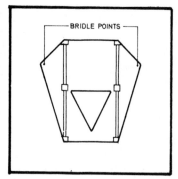

Lay spars on cover and stick down with adhesive tape

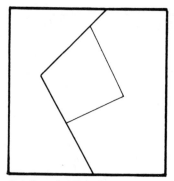

Reinforce bridle points with adhesive tape

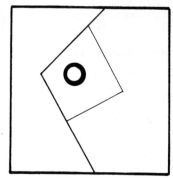

Punch bridle holes and reinforce with metal eyelets

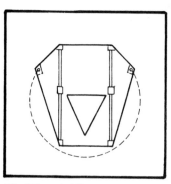

Fix 360 cm bridle as shown

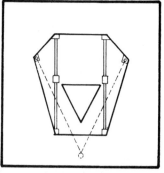

Tie knot at exact centre of bridle allowing loop for attaching flying line

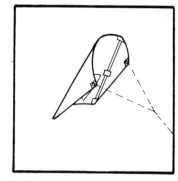

In flight

HEXAGONAL KITE

A traditional Chinese design which often carried the image of a warrior. Flies well in moderate winds

Materials required

Spars—square section hardwood or softwood
Three spars 75cm (30 in) × 0·6cm ($\frac{1}{4}$ in)

Cover 80cm (32 in) × 80cm (32 in)
Tissue paper or crepe paper

Two tails—paper streamers 300cm (120 in) × 5cm (2 in) each
Glue
Line
Towing ring

Conversions
90cm = 36 in
75cm = 30 in
15cm = 6 in

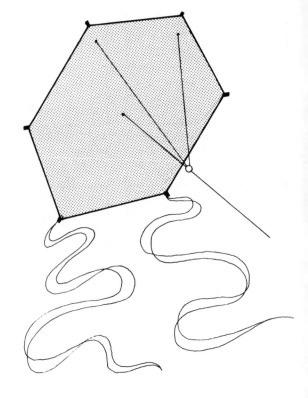

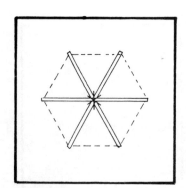

Structural form

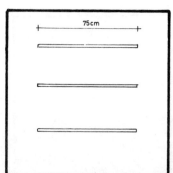

Measure spars carefully

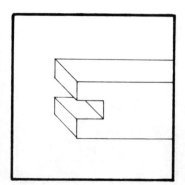

Notch ends of spars

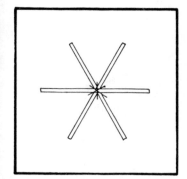

Tie spars together at centres

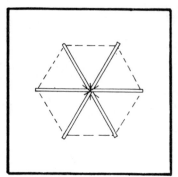

Tie line round frame, keeping ends of spars equidistant

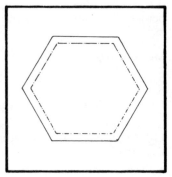

Cut out cover, allowing hem all round

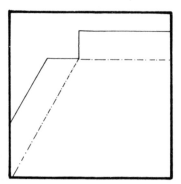

Nick corners of hem to allow turning

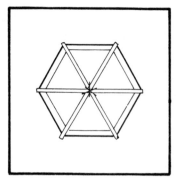

Attach cover to frame by turning and glueing down hem

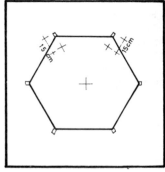

Mark 3 bridle points

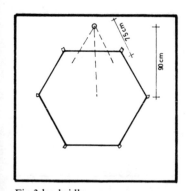

Fix 3-leg bridle

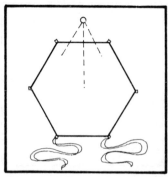

Fix 2 tails

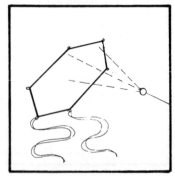

Position for launching

UMBRELLA KITE

Adapted from the Hexagonal kite, the bowing helps stability. Good flier in most winds.

Materials required

Spars—square section hardwood or softwood
Four spars 90cm (36 in) × 0·6cm (¼ in)

Cover 100cm (40 in) × 100cm (40 in)
Lightweight cloth or tissue paper or crepe paper

Three tails—paper streamers
300cm (120 in) × 5cm (2 in) each
Line
Glue
Towing ring

Conversions
90cm = 36 in
45cm = 18 in
15cm = 6 in
7·5cm = 3 in
5cm   = 2 in

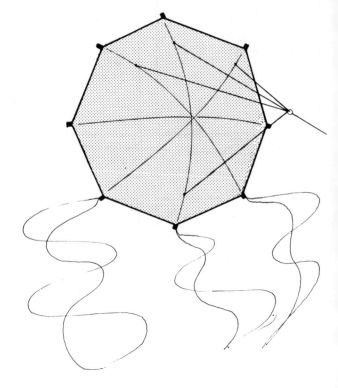

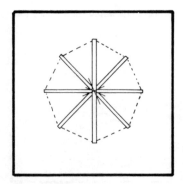

Structural form

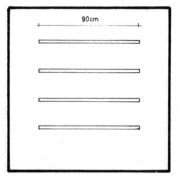

Measure spars carefully

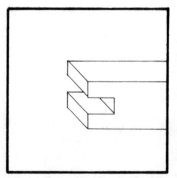

Notch ends of spars

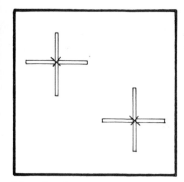

Tie pairs of spars at centres

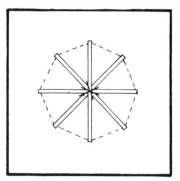

Tie spar pairs together and tie line round frame

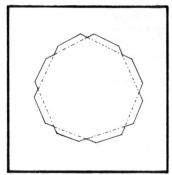

Cut out cover allowing hem all round. Nick corners of hem to allow turning

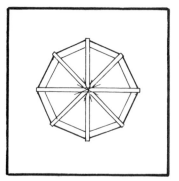

Attach cover to frame by turning over and glueing down hem

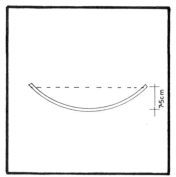

Tie line along each spar at back and tighten to bow

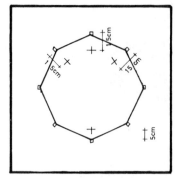

Mark 4 bridle points

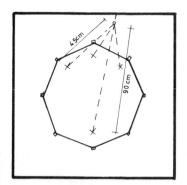

Fix 4-leg bridle. Top 3 legs of equal length

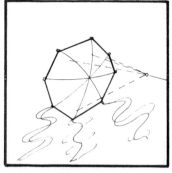

Attach 3 tails

In flight

EIGHT·POINTED STAR

A traditional Chinese design—possibly
representing a star or sun. Flies well
in moderate winds and lends itself to
elaborate decoration.

Materials required

Spars—square section hardwood
or softwood
Four spars 60cm (24 in) × 0·6cm (¼ in)

Cover 65cm (26 in) × 65cm (26 in)
Tissue paper or crepe paper
or lightweight cloth

Three tails—paper streamers 300cm (120 in)
× 5cm (2 in) each
Line
Glue
Towing ring

Conversions
75cm = 30 in
60cm = 24 in
15cm = 6 in
5cm = 2 in

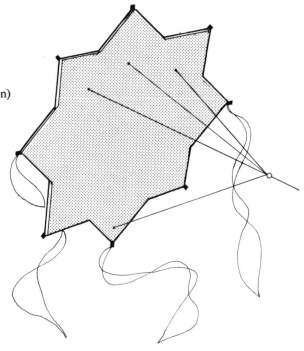

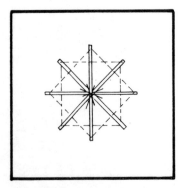

Structural form

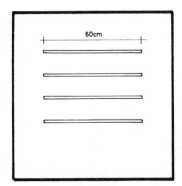

Measure spars carefully

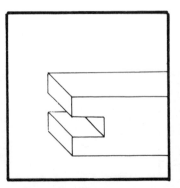

Notch ends of spars

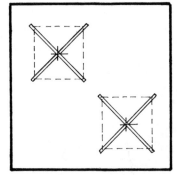

Tie spars together in pairs and tie line round each pair

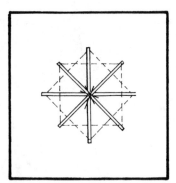

Tie pairs of spars together as shown

Fix centre joint securely with glue

Cut out cover allowing hem all round

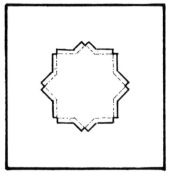

Nick corners of hem to allow turning

Attach cover to frame by turning and glueing down hem

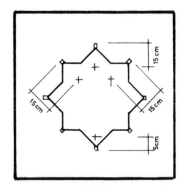

Mark 4 bridle points

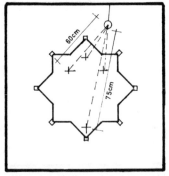

Fix 4-leg bridle. Top 3 legs of equal length

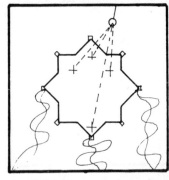

Attach 3 tails

KOREAN KITE

A traditional fighting kite, using glass-coated line for attacking an opponent's line. The hole in the centre of the kite removes the need for a tail.

Materials required

Spars—square section hardwood
or softwood or bamboo or split cane
Two spars 110cm (43 in) × 0·6cm ($\frac{1}{4}$ in)
One spar 90cm (36 in) × 0·6cm ($\frac{1}{4}$ in)
Two spars 60cm (24 in) × 0·6cm ($\frac{1}{4}$ in)

Cover 95cm (38 in) × 65cm (26 in)
Lightweight cloth or tissue paper
or crepe paper

Line
Glue
Towing ring

Conversions
110cm = 43 in
90cm = 36 in
60cm = 24 in
45cm = 18 in
23cm = 9 in
20cm = 8 in
5cm = 2 in

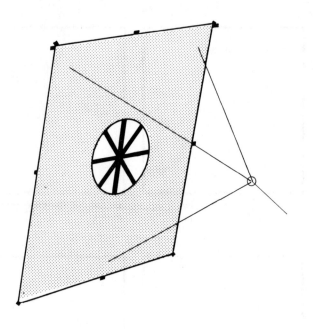

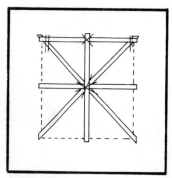

Structural form

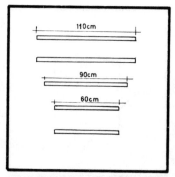

Measure spars carefully

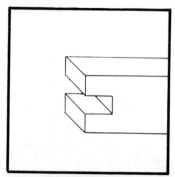

Notch ends of spars

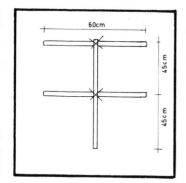

Tie horizontal spars to spine

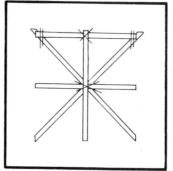

Tie diagonal cross-spars

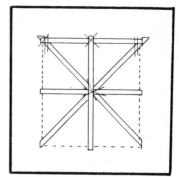

Tie line round frame

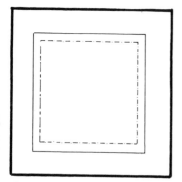

Cut out cover allowing hem all round

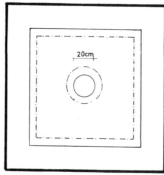

Cut hole in centre of cover

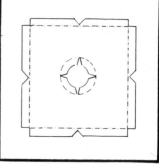

Nick corners of hem to allow turning

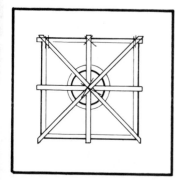

Attach cover to frame by turning and glueing down hem

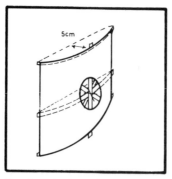

Bow both horizontal cross-spars

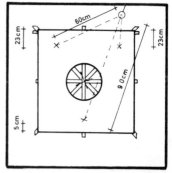

Fix 3-leg bridle. Top 2 legs of equal length

JAPANESE KITE

Traditional design representing a tree.
Like most Japanese kites it is designed
for a particular seasonal festival, in
this case the spring celebration. Flies
well in moderate winds.

Materials required

Spars—split cane or bamboo
One spar 105cm (42 in) × 0·6cm ($\frac{1}{4}$ in)
Two spars 90cm (36 in) × 0·45cm ($\frac{3}{16}$ in)
Two spars 70cm (28 in) × 0·45cm ($\frac{3}{16}$ in)
Two spars 45cm (18 in) × 0·45cm ($\frac{3}{16}$ in)

Cover 75cm (30 in) × 95cm (38 in)
Tissue paper or lightweight cloth

Tail—paper streamer 9m (30ft) × 5cm (2in)
Line
Glue
Towing ring

Conversions
125cm = 50 in
105cm = 42 in
90cm = 36 in
70cm = 28 in
65cm = 26 in
55cm = 22 in
45cm = 18 in
40cm = 16 in
30cm = 12 in
23cm = 9 in
17cm = 7 in
10cm = 4 in

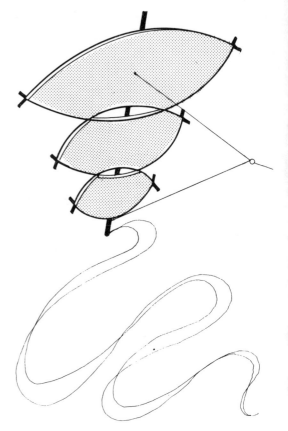

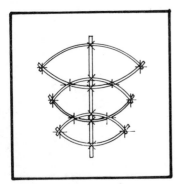

Structural form

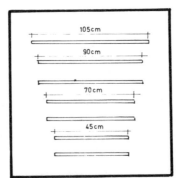

Measure spars carefully

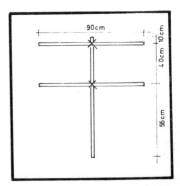

Tie spars securely on top of spine

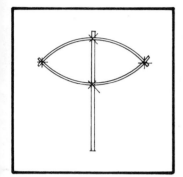

Bow together and tie securely

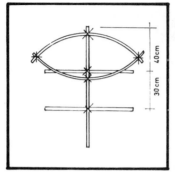

Tie second pair of spars to underside of spine

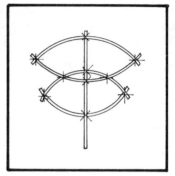

Bow spars together and tie securely

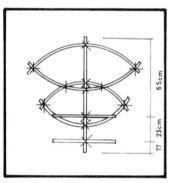

Tie third pair of spars on top of spine

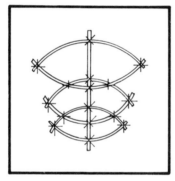

Bow spars together and tie securely

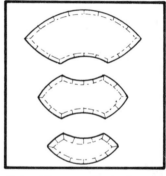

Cut out 3 covers allowing hem all round and nick hems to allow turning

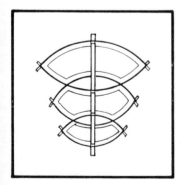

Attach covers to frame

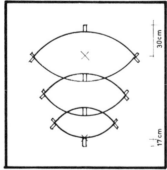

Mark 2 bridle points

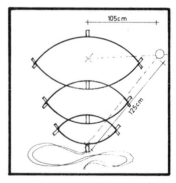

Fix 2-leg bridle and tail

NAGASAKI FIGHTING KITE

Traditional Japanese fighting kite with
excellent manoeuvrability and speed.
The line was coated with ground glass to
cut an opponent's line. Flies well in
most winds. A tail can be added for
increased stability.

Materials required

Spars—split cane or bamboo
One spar 90cm (36 in) × 0·6cm ($\frac{1}{4}$ in)
One spar 110cm (43 in) × 0·6cm ($\frac{1}{4}$ in)

Cover 100cm (40 in) × 100cm (40 in)
Lightweight cloth or tissue paper
or crepe paper

Line
Glue
Towing ring

Conversions
115cm = 46 in
110cm = 43 in
90cm = 36 in
67cm = 27 in
45cm = 18 in
23cm = 9 in
5cm   = 2 in

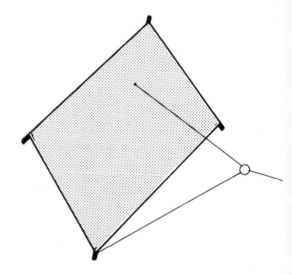

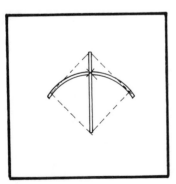

Structural form

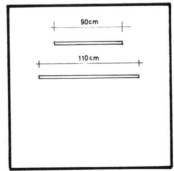

Measure spars carefully

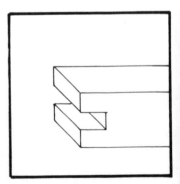

Notch ends of spars

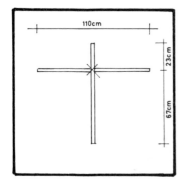

Tie cross-spar to spine

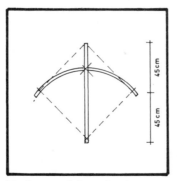

Tie line round frame bowing cross-spar till ends are level with centre of spine

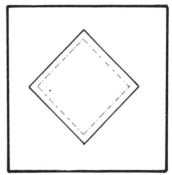

Cut out cover allowing hem all round

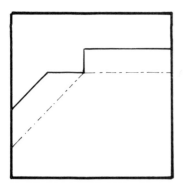

Nick corners of hem to allow turning

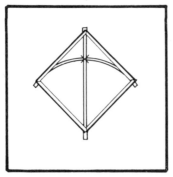

Attach cover to frame by turning and glueing down hem

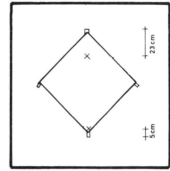

Mark 2 bridle points

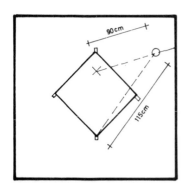

Fix 2-leg bridle

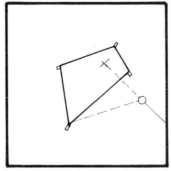

Position for launching

Kites in flight

AEROPLANE KITE

The Western innovation of the fin gives
this kite increased stability, acting like
the keel of a boat. Flies well at a
great height in moderate winds.

Materials required

Spars—square section hardwood
or softwood or bamboo
One spar 120cm (48 in) × 0·6cm ($\frac{1}{4}$ in)
One spar 90cm (36 in) × 0·6cm ($\frac{1}{4}$ in)
One spar 60cm (24 in) × 0·6cm ($\frac{1}{4}$ in)
One spar 20cm (8 in) × 0·6cm ($\frac{1}{4}$ in)

Cover 95cm (38 in) × 125cm (49 in)
Lightweight cloth or tissue paper
or crepe paper

Cloth adhesive tape
Line
Glue
Towing ring

Conversions
120cm = 48 in
90cm = 36 in
60cm = 24 in
45cm = 18 in
36cm = 14 in
30cm = 12 in
20cm = 8 in
15cm = 6 in

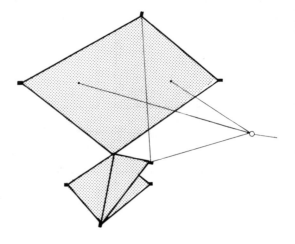

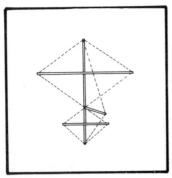

Structural form

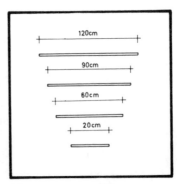

Measure spars carefully

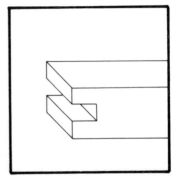

Notch ends of spars, but one end
only of shortest

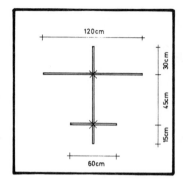

Tie wing spars to spine

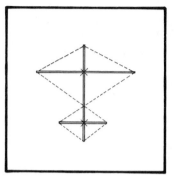

Tie line round frame as shown

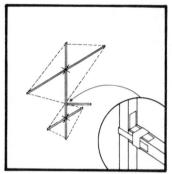

Fix fin spar to spine where lines cross, using cloth adhesive tape

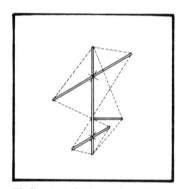

Tie line to hold fin spar steady

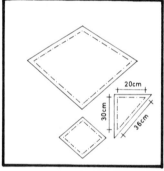

Cut out covers allowing hem all round

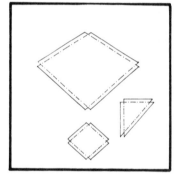

Nick corners of hem to allow turning

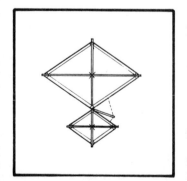

Attach main covers to frame by turning and glueing down hem

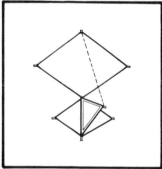

Attach fin cover

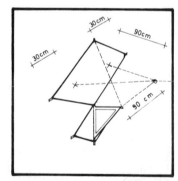

Fix 3-leg bridle. Top two legs of equal length

PYRAMID KITE

Developed by Alexander Graham Bell at
the turn of the century as part of his
experiments into manflight. Flies well
in high winds.

Materials required

Spars—square section hardwood
or softwood
Six spars 75cm (30 in) × 0·6cm (¼ in)
Cover 160cm (64 in) × 80cm (32 in)
Lightweight cloth or tissue paper
or crepe paper

Line
Glue
Towing ring

Conversions
150cm = 60 in
75cm = 30 in
60cm = 24 in

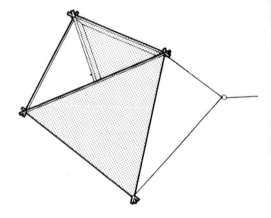

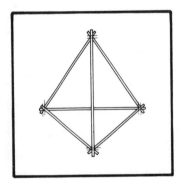

Structural form

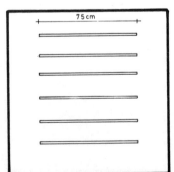

Measure spars carefully

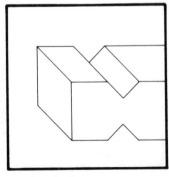

Notch ends of spars

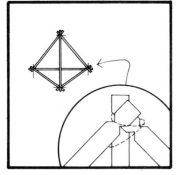

Tie spars firmly together making
pyramid shape

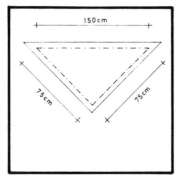

Cut out cover allowing hem
all round

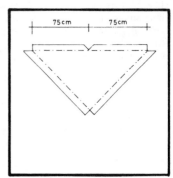

Nick corners of hem to allow
turning

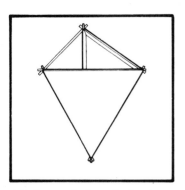

Attach cover to frame by turning
and glueing down hem

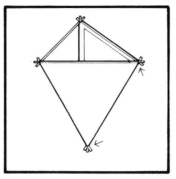

Mark 2 bridle points

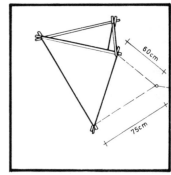

Fix 2-leg bridle

BOX KITE

Invented by Hargraves in Australia in the late nineteenth century and was used as part of the R.A.F. Sea Rescue equipment for carrying wireless aerials. Very stable in moderate and heavy winds.

Materials required

Spars—square section hardwood or softwood
Four spars 90cm (36 in) × 0·6cm (¼ in)
Four spars 43cm (17 in) × 0·6cm (¼ in)

Cover 137cm (54 in) × 70cm (28 in)
Lightweight cloth

Needle and cotton
Line
Glue

Conversions

133cm = 53 in
90cm = 36 in
43cm = 17 in
30cm = 12 in
23cm = 9 in
15cm = 6 in
10cm = 4 in
2·5cm = 1 in
0·6cm = ¼ in

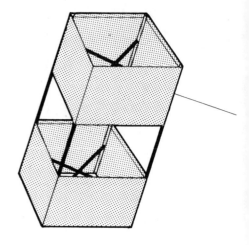

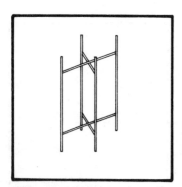

Structural form

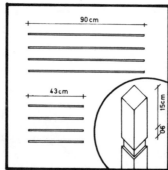

Measure spars carefully and notch both ends of long spars as shown

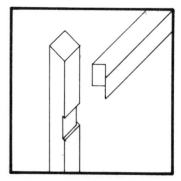

Notch ends of cross-spars to fit notches in long spars

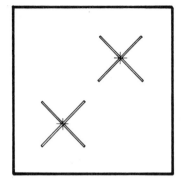

Tie pairs of cross-spars at centres

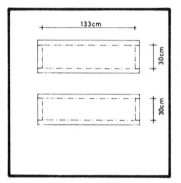

Cut covers allowing hems. Turn and sew down top and bottom hems of each cover

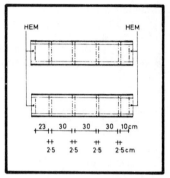

Mark position of long spar pockets

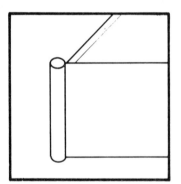

Sew each pocket as shown, allowing room to hold long spar

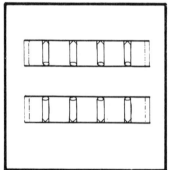

Stitch closed one end of each pocket as shown

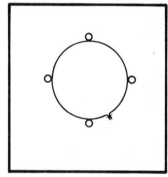

Sew together ends of each cover keeping pockets equidistant

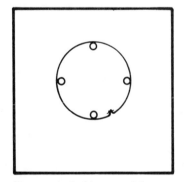

Turn covers inside out and insert long spars

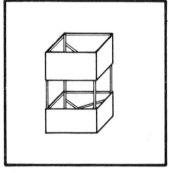

Slit pockets over cross-spar notches. Push cross-spars into place

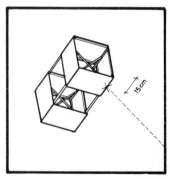

Attach flying line to tying point

BIRD KITE

Adapted from traditional Chinese/Malaysian design. It hovers at a great height looking like a bird of prey and is sometimes used by Eastern farmers as a bird scare. Flies well in moderate winds.

Materials required

Spars—square section hardwood or softwood or split cane or bamboo
One spar 110cm (44 in) × 0·6cm (¼ in)
Two spars 90cm (36 in) × 0·6cm (¼ in)
One spar 17cm (7 in) × 0·6cm (¼ in)

Cover 90cm (36 in) × 90cm (36 in)
Lightweight cloth or crepe paper or tissue paper

Two tails—paper streamers 12m (40 ft) × 5cm (2 in) each
Line
Glue
Towing ring

Conversions
120cm = 48 in
110cm = 44 in
90cm = 36 in
70cm = 28 in
45cm = 18 in
30cm = 12 in
20cm = 8 in
17cm = 7 in

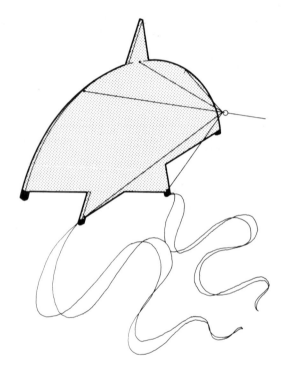

Structural form

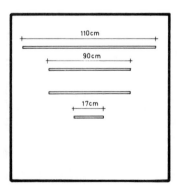

Measure spars carefully

Tie spars together at one end. See detail

Detail. Spar ends must be shaved down to ensure neat mitre joint, then glue and tie

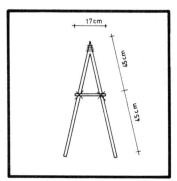

Tie short spar as shown

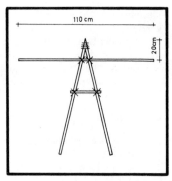

Tie wing spar across frame as shown

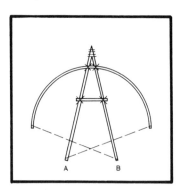

Bow wing spar by tying back to points A and B

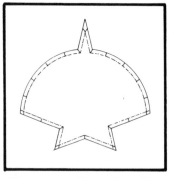

Cut out cover allowing hem all round and nick hem to allow turning

Attach cover to frame by turning and glueing down hem

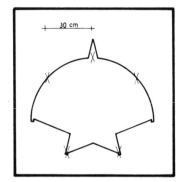

Mark 5 bridle points

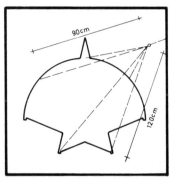

Fix 5-leg bridle. Top 3 legs and bottom 2 legs of equal length

Attach two tails

MARCONI KITE

Developed by Marconi the inventor of the
wireless, and used in his famous first
intercontinental radio link-up to carry
the aerial. A difficult kite to make
well but is capable of fine adjustment and
is a very efficient flying machine. Flies
in moderate to heavy winds.

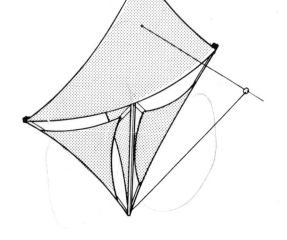

Materials required

Spars—square section hardwood
or softwood
Two spars 120cm (48 in) × 0·6cm ($\frac{1}{4}$ in)
One spar 20cm (8 in) × 0·6cm ($\frac{1}{4}$ in)

Cover 120cm (48 in) × 120cm (48 in)
Lightweight cloth
Twelve tabs 15cm (6 in) × 0·6cm ($\frac{1}{4}$ in) each
Cotton tape
Cloth-reinforced adhesive tape
Needle and cotton
Line, Glue and Towing ring

Conversions

120cm = 48 in
90cm = 36 in
85cm = 34 in
78cm = 31 in
55cm = 22 in
30cm = 12 in
20cm = 8 in
15cm = 6 in
7·5cm = 3 in
5cm = 2 in

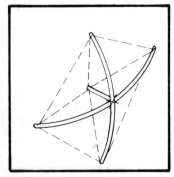

Structural form

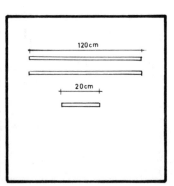

120cm

20cm

Measure spars carefully

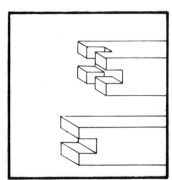

Notch ends of long spars and
cross-notch one end only of
short spar

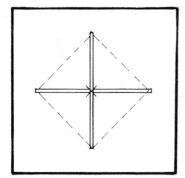

Tie long spars together at centres and tie line round frame

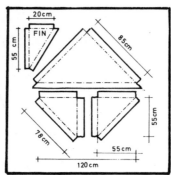

Cut out covers allowing hems all round and nick all corners to allow turning

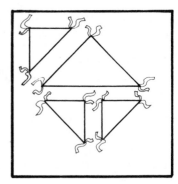

Turn under and sew down hems. Stitch on tabs for fixing covers to frame

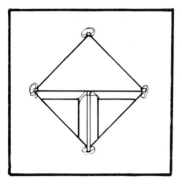

Lie covers over frame to ensure correct fit. Do not attach yet.

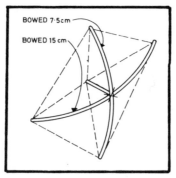

Fix fin spar to back of kite as in next diagram and bow spars as shown

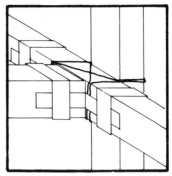

Fix fin spar to spine using cloth-reinforced adhesive tape

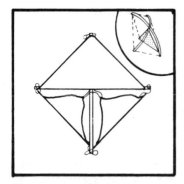

Tie on covers, including fin cover at back

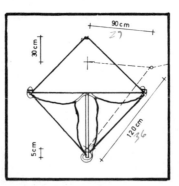

Fix 2-leg bridle

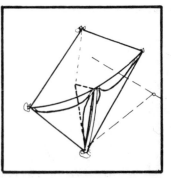

Bottom flaps should be loose in light winds and tight in heavy winds. Main cover and fin cover always tight

TRIANGULATED BOX KITE

Adapted from Hargraves Box Kite.
It is stable in heavy winds.

Materials required

Spars—square section hardwood
or softwood
Three spars 90cm (36 in) × 0·6cm ($\frac{1}{4}$ in)
Six spars 38cm (15 in) × 0·6cm ($\frac{1}{4}$ in)

Cover 115cm (46 in) × 65cm (26 in)
Lightweight cloth
Twelve tabs 15cm (6 in) × 0·6cm
($\frac{1}{4}$ in) each. Cotton tape

Needle and cotton

Line
Glue

Conversions

115cm = 46 in
90cm = 36 in
38cm = 15 in
27cm = 11 in
23cm = 9 in
15cm = 6 in
12cm = 5 in
10cm = 4 in
2cm   = 1 in
1cm   = $\frac{1}{2}$ in

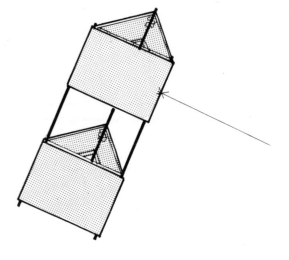

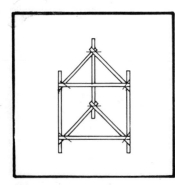

Structural form

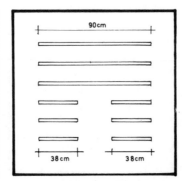

Measure spars carefully

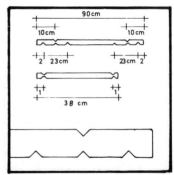

Notch ends of all spars as shown

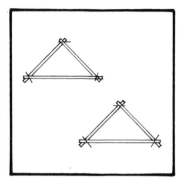

Tie short spars together to form 2 triangles

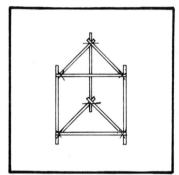

Tie triangles to vertical spars. Glue joints

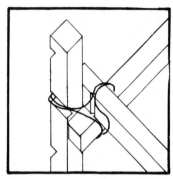

Detail. Triangles tied to vertical spars

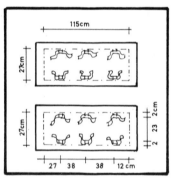

Cut out covers allowing hem all round. Stitch down hems, sew on tabs as shown

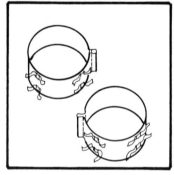

Sew ends of covers together to fit kite frame firmly with tabs outside

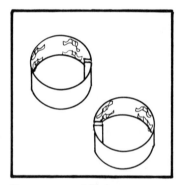

Turn covers outside in

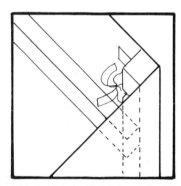

Tie on covers with tabs round notches

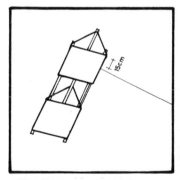

Fix flying line to tying point

In flight

CONYNE KITE

The Conyne kite, named after its inventor Silas J. Conyne, is sometimes called the French Military kite, because it was first used by the French army during the 1914–18 war. The kite is made up of plane and angled surfaces. It is a good medium- to heavy-weather kite and will fly in winds of 10 to 25 knots

Materials required

Spars—square section hardwood or softwood
Four spars 100cm (40 in) × 0·6cm ($\frac{1}{4}$ in)
One spar 30cm (12 in) × 0·6cm ($\frac{1}{4}$ in)

Cover 120cm (48 in) × 120cm (48 in)
Lightweight cloth

Pockets 30cm (12 in) × 30cm (12 in)
lightweight canvas or reinforced nylon

Needle and cotton
Line
Towing ring

Conversions

135cm	= 54 in	33cm	= 13 in
106cm	= 42 in	30cm	= 12 in
100cm	= 40 in	27.5cm	= 11 in
70cm	= 28 in	15cm	= 6 in
55cm	= 22 in	5cm	= 2 in
40cm	= 16 in	2·5cm	= 1 in
38cm	= 15 in		

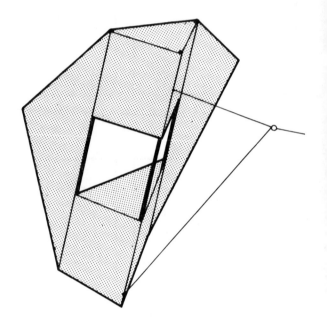

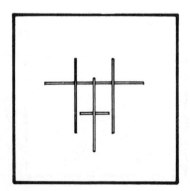

Structural form

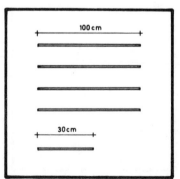

Measure spars carefully

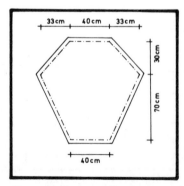

Cut out main cover allowing hem all round

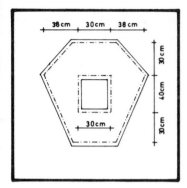

Cut out central hole allowing hem all round

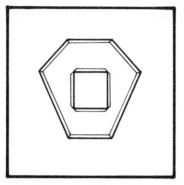

Nick all corners of hems. Then turn over and sew down hems

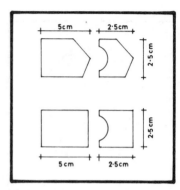

Cut out canvas pocket shapes— 4 of each

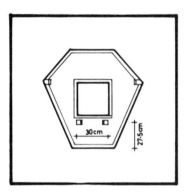

Mark position of spar pockets on back of cover and sew down firmly. See detail

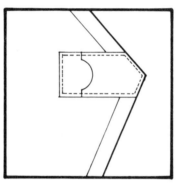

Detail of spar pockets

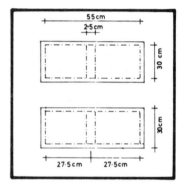

Cut out small covers and mark positions for central spar pocket

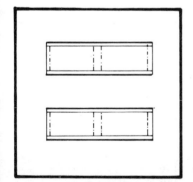

Turn over and sew down top and bottom hems of each small cover

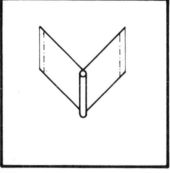

Sew central spar pocket to hold spar firmly

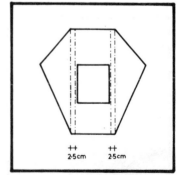

Mark positions of long spar pockets on front of main cover

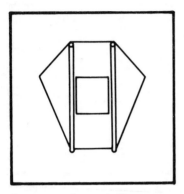

Sew spar pockets to hold spars firmly

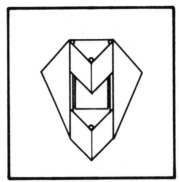

Sew small covers to main cover. See detail

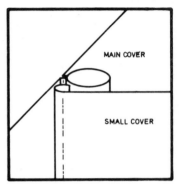

MAIN COVER

SMALL COVER

Detail of how to sew small cover to main cover

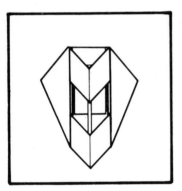

Insert all long spars and sew pocket ends closed

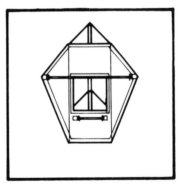

Insert horizontal spars across back of main cover

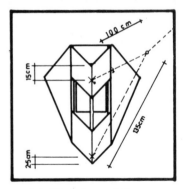

Mark bridle points and fix 2-leg bridle

MULTICELL TETRAHEDRAL KITE

This is an extended version of the single-cell kite and can be extended still further. Alexander Graham Bell built a kite with many hundreds of cells. Needs a high wind for good flight.

Materials required

Spars—square section hardwood or softwood
Seven spars 140cm (56 in) × 0·6cm (¼ in)
Twelve spars 67cm (27 in) × 0·6cm (¼ in)

Cover 530cm (216 in) × 85cm (33 in)
Lightweight cloth

Corner brackets 0·3cm (⅛ in) plywood
Approx. 30cm (12 in) × 30cm (12 in)

Panel pins
Cloth-reinforced adhesive 5cm (2 in) tape
Line, Glue and Towing ring

Conversions
140cm = 56 in
125cm = 50 in
100cm = 40 in
70cm = 28 in

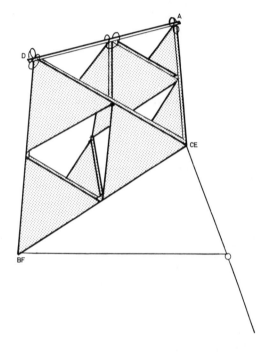

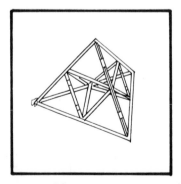

Structural form

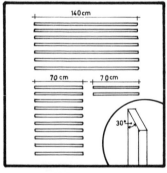

Measure spars carefully and mitre all ends to an angle of 30°

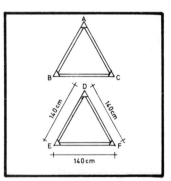

Join long spars to form 2 triangles. See detail

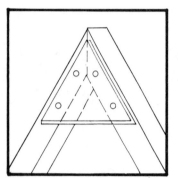

Detail. Cut corner brackets and glue and pin to spars

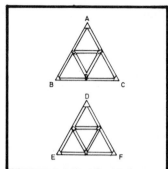

Attach internal spars as shown. See detail

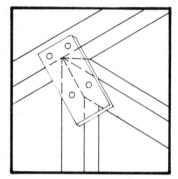

Detail. Cut corner brackets and glue and pin to spars

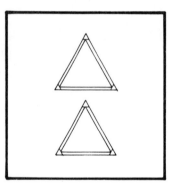

Make up remaining spars into 2 triangles. See detail

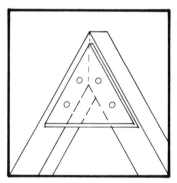

Detail. Cut corner brackets and glue and pin to spars.

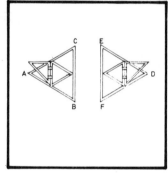

Using adhesive tape attach triangles to main frames as shown. See detail

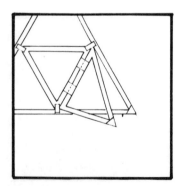

Detail of adhesive tape hinge

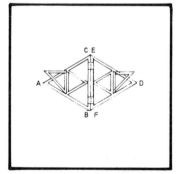

Hinge main frames together as shown. See detail

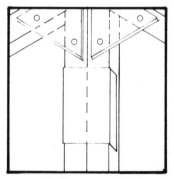

Detail of adhesive tape hinge

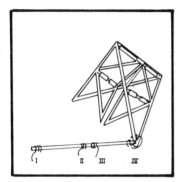

Tie remaining long spar to main frame as shown. See details

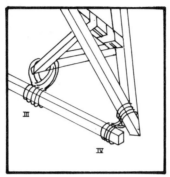

Detail of tying long spar to main frame

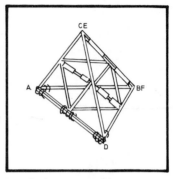

Detail of structure without cover showing long spar tied to frame

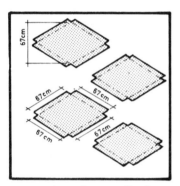

Cut out 4 equal covers allowing hems all round

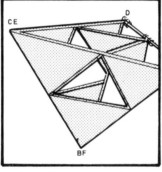

Tack or glue covers turning hems round spars

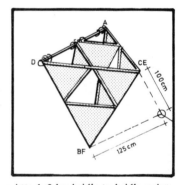

Attach 2-leg bridle to bridle points